In the UK it is called football. In America it is called soccer. But whether we call it football or soccer, the game and the rules are the same. Football is played more than any other game.

Football is played by two teams of eleven players. Each team has its own strip, so it is easy to tell the two teams apart. The strip consists of a shirt, shorts and socks.

Each club has a home strip and one, or more, away strips. An away strip is used if a team is playing at another team's ground and their two strips look the same.

The aim in a game of football is to get the ball into the other team's net, and so score a goal. The team who has more goals at the end of the match is the winner.

It is the goalkeeper's job to stop the other team from scoring goals. The goalkeeper is the only player allowed to touch the ball with his hands but only when he is in the penalty box.

goal

Soccer is played on a pitch, marked out with white lines. At each end of the pitch is the goal net.

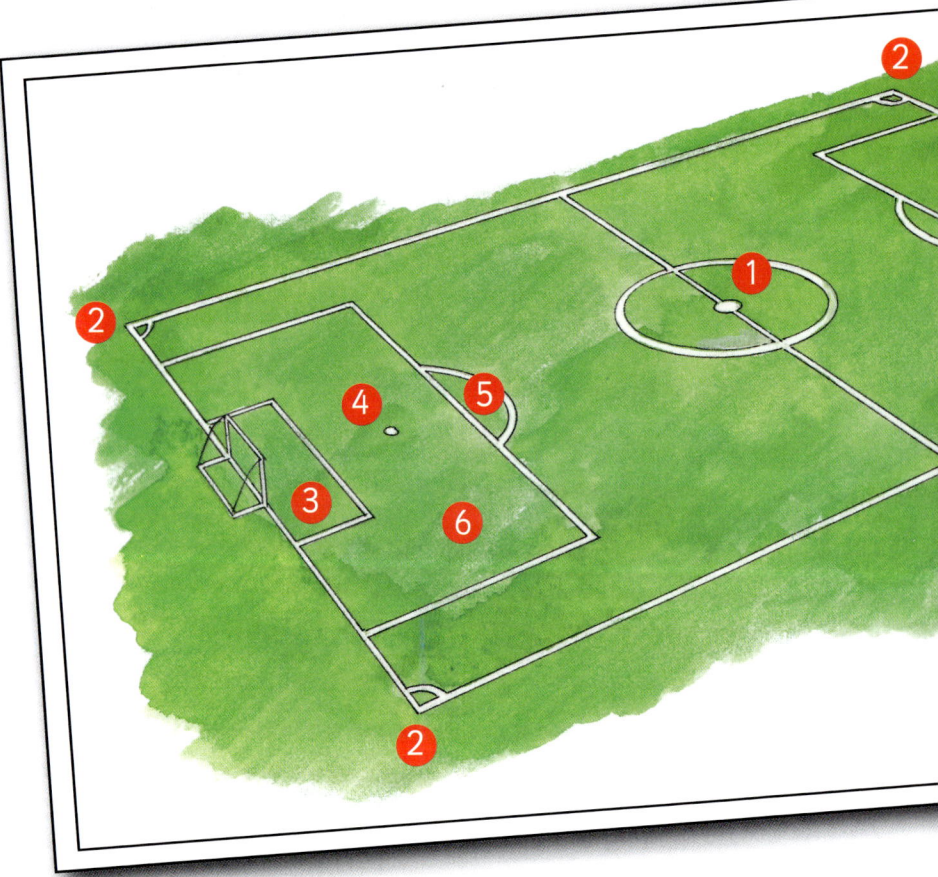

① The ball is put here at the start of a game or when a goal has been scored.

② Corner kicks are taken here, the corner arc.

③ This is the six-yard box. The goalkeeper takes a goal kick from here.

④ The penalty spot is where the ball is put for a penalty kick.

⑤ This is the penalty arc. Players cannot stand here when a penalty is taken.

⑥ The penalty box.

whistle

flag

The referee normally has a black shirt and shorts. He checks that the players follow the rules of the game. There are assistant referees on the sides of the pitch, who help the referee on the pitch.

The referee blows a whistle to tell players what to do. He and his assistants make signals with their arms to show players, and supporters, what has happened or what will happen next.

referee

It is a very difficult job. Players and supporters sometimes disagree with the referee and argue with him.

red card

The referee has two cards. One is red and the other is yellow. If a player does something wrong, like tripping up another player or holding his shirt, it is called a foul. If this happens, the other team could get a free kick.

If a foul is committed in the penalty box, the other team get a penalty kick. The ball is put on the penalty spot and a player kicks it at the goal.

Only the goalkeeper, referee and the player kicking the ball are allowed in the penalty box, until the ball has been kicked.

If players commit a foul, they could be given a yellow card, or booked. This means they have their name written down in the referee's book. The referee holds up the yellow card so everyone can see it.

yellow card

If a player commits a very bad foul, or keeps on fouling other players, he or she could be shown a red card and be sent off the pitch.

If this happens, the team cannot put another player on and they have to continue the game without the player who was sent off.

the 1800s

Games similar to soccer have been played for hundreds, if not thousands, of years. In some games, teams could have as many players as they wanted. Games were played in the streets, not on pitches. In the 1800s, a set of rules was agreed and written down.

The first balls were made of pigs' bladders that had been blown up, or from animal skins, stuffed and made into a round shape.

Until the 1940s, the balls were made from leather, and they were very heavy. If it rained, the ball would get heavier and slower, and it would be very difficult to play with.

At first, the teams wore caps so everyone could tell which team the player belonged to. Today, players are given a cap if they play for their country. If a player has been capped five times, it means he or she has played for his or her country five times.

cap